FOREWORD

In the eight years that we have worked with the 4-Blocks framework, hundreds of teachers, consultants, and administrators have come to visit in the classrooms and talk with us about implementation issues. Of all the people we have talked to and observed as they helped teachers implement this framework in their classrooms, Cheryl Sigmon is far and away the best! In her role with the South Carolina State Department of Education, she has spent hundreds of days meeting with, coaching, and observing in the classrooms of teachers. She has figured out what materials were needed and helped teachers get them. She has noticed the problems teachers had when they first began implementation and helped them avoid or overcome these. Cheryl has also worked extensively with administrators and helped them learn how to evaluate and support the successful implementation of the framework.

This guide is a result of all her tireless efforts with teachers and administrators. Cheryl sent us an early draft of this guide to comment on and we immediately began to look for ways to get it published and available to everyone working to implement the framework. Many a good educational idea has been abandoned because the implementation captured the letter—but not the strength—of the original model. We are indebted to Cheryl for her thoughtful and inspired work.

Dorothy P. Hall

Pat Cunningham

INTRODUCTION

As a consultant serving teachers through an in-class model of assistance, I was often as equally frustrated as the teachers with whom I was working as we looked for solutions to familiar problems. One frustrating problem was in trying to attend to the individual needs of students in heterogeneous classes during guided reading. I felt like the performer I witnessed once on the old Ed Sullivan Show who kept a dozen plates spinning on dowel rods by frantically running from plate to plate to keep them rotating. Try as I might, in my classroom demonstrations there was no way to make my modeling appear effortless, because it wasn't. Additionally, while I could feel some confidence that eventually throughout the day I would meet the needs of each child, I was finally convinced that their needs just could not be met simultaneously.

The day that I heard Pat Cunningham describe the 4-Blocks Model was my salvation! What I had once thought impossible was made so clear to me. Not one day since being introduced to the 4-Blocks Model have I lacked confidence that individual needs of students—even in classrooms with tremendous diversity—can be met in the language arts classroom with all students engaged in meaningful, productive learning activities.

Since my introduction to the model, I have had the opportunity to work with Pat Cunningham and Dottie Hall and with many of the teachers in the schools where the model is well-established to learn all that I could about the ins and outs of the model. I have had the experience of working alongside teachers as they implemented the model. I have had opportunities to teach the blocks to students to find out exactly what teachers face throughout the day in management and delivery of the model. I have witnessed teacher after teacher discover the model and the wondrous difference it makes to them and to their students—ALL of their students. No longer do I and the teachers I work with need to run fast, furiously, and futilely to "keep all of the plates spinning" to be successful in the classroom. The 4-Blocks Model is manageable, even for those of us who don't feel exceptionally well-organized, and it has truly changed the way many of us think about teaching and learning.

In this book, I have tried to share what I have learned from listening carefully, from watching observantly, and from a great deal of experimenting through trial and error. Although trial and error is not a bad way to learn, I hope that the shortcuts offered to you in this book will have your model running quickly and smoothly so that you and your students will discover, as soon as possible, the joys of teaching and learning in a 4-Blocks classroom. Since not a great deal has been published about this model, there is often confusion among teachers and administrators about the blocks, the purpose of the blocks, and the way that they operate. I have attempted to offer assistance both to teachers and administrators that may make implementation easier and more successful.

Teachers need an outline of the essential elements of the model as a guideline for implementation, which is found within this book. Additionally, teachers must make many critical decisions in planning effectively for each of the blocks for which this book offers assistance.

This book also serves as a valuable resource for administrators in their role, both in and out of the classroom, which is necessary for success. Administrators will find suggestions within this book for planning staff development, which may be different from staff development plans prior to implementation of 4-Blocks. Not only may this model change how you view teaching and learning, but also how you view professional development. A number of paradigms must change for implementation; however, once changed, you'll never want to return to the old way of doing things.

May your experience with 4-Blocks be truly wonderful and rewarding—for you and your students!

TABLE OF CONTENTS

PUTTING IT ALL TOGETHER

ABOUT STAFF DEVELOPMENT

MYTH:

Attending a conference or institute means that an attendee is fully trained and is a qualified trainer.

FACT:

During a three-day institute about the 4-Blocks Literacy Model, an attendee usually learns the basics of the model and the underlying philosophy of each of the Blocks. As implementation begins, a great deal of support is necessary to continue to grow and understand the model. This model is consistent with research in effective staff development. Gone are the days of designing staff development programs of an hour, a half day, or whole day, or even of multiple-day workshops with the expectation of having sweeping, long-lasting effects.

Interviews with teachers who have had at least one to two years of experience with the model, revealed growth through the following statements:

"Learning about 4-Blocks was not just about finding a new way to teach. We learned a lot about how children learn and specifically about how kids learn to read. The training was beneficial whether or not the model was adopted."

"Even in the first month, I could tell that my year was going to be a good one. Somehow through my initial training I had gained a clearer purpose and clearer goals for my teaching."

MODELS OF IMPLEMENTATION AT STATE, DISTRICT, AND SCHOOL LEVELS

Implementing the 4-Blocks Model usually requires designing a long-term staff development plan and further requires making a substantial commitment towards focused, collaborative professional growth. Gone are the days when a one-shot in-service program of an hour, a half-day, or even of a couple of days will support the kinds of changes that will make a real difference in classrooms. **To most school faculties, the 4-Blocks Model will mean absorbing a whole new philosophy about teaching and learning, building networks of support to work through successes and failures during implementation, and redesigning master schedules to accommodate the model.**

Whole language probably did as much as any past educational movement to reeducate people about what is really necessary to effect permanent changes in teaching. In schools where whole language was deemed successful, faculties spent, and are likely still spending, quality time studying, discussing, refining, focusing, coaching, and practicing to understand the philosophy and to perfect their classroom delivery. In schools which failed to see positive achievement gains, training was often far too brief. Consequently, many teachers never fully understood or absorbed the philosophy (or else phonics instruction would not have become dichotomous with whole language); teachers became frustrated in their attempts to implement and had little or no support to correct and strengthen their attempts, and abandonment became the final solution.

Educators, of all professionals, should learn from past mistakes. Failing at one method should not mean returning to a previous method which was equally unsuccessful or with which they were less than satisfied. Too much research exists which can help schools to improve their methods and performance. **The 4-Blocks Model is based on solid practices of proven success backed by data.** The model is worth an attempt if a school or district has data that indicate that it may not be meeting the needs of all students or that all students are not performing to their potential. Moving into implementation, however, needs serious consideration as it will require long-term, on-going, sustained training.

The attitude that a state, district, or school should adopt in moving towards making substantial change, as with implementation of the 4-Blocks Model, is that the long-term, training and implementation can be a wonderful opportunity for true professional collaboration and growth. Embarking in the process and sustaining that spirit can be the greatest experience in which a school or district has ever engaged. Additionally encouraging with the 4-Blocks Model, results of current initiatives even after six months to a year have provided the impetus to continue with renewed enthusiasm.

Suggested designs of training for the 4-Blocks Model which have been proven successful are briefly outlined on the following pages.

One state has successfully initiated two different models of implementation, directed at two different purposes and two different populations. Both are viable models.

1. Pilot for a Small Number of Low-Achieving Districts

    This project was limited in scope as a result of the limited number of support personnel involved in the project. One Department of Education consultant coordinated the staff development and provided direct, in-classroom assistance; hence, even within the few districts involved, the available time, money, and manpower were further concentrated towards supporting lead teachers. In this pilot project, five districts formed a consortium coordinated by a consultant from the Department of Education. These five districts were involved in a planned program of assistance as a result of below standard performance on a number of measures. The districts chose to focus their efforts on making changes in classroom instruction to impact language arts and literacy skills, particularly in reading. Most of their students in these districts qualified for free and reduced lunch (about 90% or higher in several of the districts). The five districts agreed to pool their resources—financial and manpower—towards achieving their goals to increase literacy levels. The plan devised and executed is summarized as follows:

    Goals for First Year of Plan: To acquaint all primary teachers and their administrators with the 4-Blocks Model; To identify lead teachers at each of the schools involved who would receive in-depth training opportunities; To begin to establish model classrooms with lead teachers; To equip lead teachers with materials necessary to implement the model; To provide necessary support for teachers during stages of implementation.

    Plan of Action:

    *   All primary teachers and administrators attended a three day institute coordinated by the Department of Education prior to the beginning of school.
    *   Lead teachers were identified by their administrators for each first and second grade at each school involved in the initiative.
    *   Department of Education consultant met at least monthly with lead teachers at each school.
    *   Department of Education consultant took lead teachers to schools out of state to observe successful 4-Blocks programs.
    *   Department of Education consultant worked with district and school administrators to order appropriate materials for lead teachers, especially books necessary to implement Guided Reading Block and Self-Selected Reading Block.
    *   Teachers and administrators attended a mid-year institute coordinated by Department of Education to get further information about varying strategies in the blocks and to ask questions necessary to support continued implementation.
    *   Department of Education consultant provided in-class assistance in the manner of demonstrations, coaching, and team-teaching.
    *   Other teachers in the schools began to visit lead teachers as the lead teachers became comfortable with the model. They began to serve as mentors for their co-workers in their implementation efforts.

- Teachers and administrators attended a third institute to conclude the first year's cycle of training. Successes and failures were discussed; new strategies were shared, and questions were answered.

Results of the First Cycle of Training:

Data on standardized tests administered varied greatly, though were generally positive. In one of the small districts, where support was strongest and implementation guidelines were followed closely, increases in student achievement in the areas of language and reading were phenomenal. The numbers of students who had previously scored in the bottom quarter were cut in half. There was a dramatic increase of students moving into the next highest quarter. Besides the increase in test scores, teachers who had implemented all of the blocks in the model reported that they were convinced that their students were better, more proficient readers and writers than ever before. That was the most convincing documentation that the model had been successful. Additionally noteworthy was the fact that all five districts have continued to focus on and support the model.

2. Pilot for All Interested Districts in a State

This model of implementation involved an invitation from the Department of Education in one state to each of its districts to participate in a training program for the 4-Blocks Model. Each district elected a team from one of their elementary schools comprised of the following members: two first grade teachers, two second grade teachers, their building level administrator, and a person appointed by the district as the mentor. The mentor was to have been a person who did not have full-time classroom responsibilities for the purpose of having time during the school day to coach teachers during implementation and to help replicate the model in other classrooms and in other schools in the district should the district be interested in expanding the model.

Goals for Statewide Training: To make training available to all school districts in response to the demand for this training; To assist districts in replicating the model by establishing model classrooms, lead teachers, and mentors from which other district personnel could learn; To assure quality training in the state; To correct existing misconceptions about the model in the state; To offer schools a non-commercial, research-based literacy model to help teachers deal effectively with heterogeneous groups of students; To offer districts an alternative balanced approach to teaching reading/language arts; To demonstrate an on-going, sustained model of professional development.

Plan of Action:

- Two cycles of training were planned to accommodate the large number of participants. Each participant received eight days of intensive training, and mentors received three additional days for a total of eleven days. Additional networks of support were planned such as schools to visit, on-line assistance, and periodical, interactive teleconferences.

- The training days, whether eight or eleven, were distributed across a number of months so that questions could be answered and support could be offered at strategic points during implementation. Training was designed to allow time between sessions for participants to try strategies.

- Topics for the training and the sequence in which they were included were as follows:

    - Philosophy of the 4-Blocks Model
    - Overview of Each of the Blocks Demonstrations and Discussions of Each of the Blocks
    - Starting the Year with the Model
    - Make and Take Materials Necessary for the Model
    - Administering IRIs
    - Connecting the Model to the State Frameworks and Achievement Standards
    - Administrator's Role in Implementation
    - Effective Coaching and Feedback for Improvement
    - Varying Strategies in the Blocks
    - Adaptations of the Model for Other Grade Levels (K and 3+)
    - Establishing Networks of Support for Teachers and Administrators

- For much of the training, successful classroom teachers were used as presenters, especially for demonstration lessons and for answering questions concerning day-to-day operations and management. The ratio of participants to trainer/facilitators was usually kept at 30:1 to ensure that training was as interactive as possible.

- All teams were invited to come to the initial two day presentation to hear the philosophy of the model and an overview of each of the blocks. After that presentation, districts that wished to continue with the training were asked to sign an assurance form agreeing to comply with guidelines that would serve to assure them greater success. Guidelines included such items as the following: 1) All six team members would attend each training session; 2) Teachers would agree to receive administrators and mentors in their classes for observations and to accept feedback about their implementation; 3) The school would furnish the four teachers who were a part of their team all basic materials required for the model (a list of the basic materials was included); and many other guidelines.

- To ensure that the training was as uniform as possible, calibration training sessions were held with all facilitator/trainers prior to each of the actual training days with participants.

Results of Statewide Training:

The training cycles have not been completed at the publication of this book; however, feedback from districts has been quite positive.

9

District Support for the 4-Blocks Model

The plan for initiating training from the district level can be similar to the state-level advocacy plan. District curriculum personnel should consider the following questions before designing their plan.

How many schools should be involved and how much oversight will the implementation require? Who will provide the most direct assistance?

- If several schools in the district are in great need of substantial, programmatic change, the training and assistance may need to be limited only to those.

- If a district is aware that a great deal of professional growth will need to occur with the teaching staff in order to make substantial changes in the curriculum and instruction, then the number of schools may need to be limited. If the majority of the faculty members in the district's schools readily accept change and quickly absorb new material, then more schools may be successfully trained at the same time

- If the schools involved have strong instructional leaders who can be active supporters of the teachers throughout implementation, more schools can be trained with fewer district office personnel needed to provide direct support.

Do trainers have necessary credentials and experience with the model?

- Districts need to choose trainers wisely. Presently, no certification program exists for the 4-Blocks training. Potential trainers need to elaborate on how, when, and by whom they received their training and what experiences they have had with practical application of the model. Merely reading books on the subject would not constitute sufficient training, nor would having attended one institute of two or three days.

Can the assigned district staff members and the school level administrators commit enough of their own time and of their planned professional development days to focus on the model and its components?

- As much available time as possible should be allocated towards growing with the model. Formal staff development days are not the only opportunity for faculty members to receive professional training: faculty meetings; grade-level planning time at specified intervals; special interest groups meeting before school, during lunch, or after school; and other available times can be productive in continuing to sustain the implementation.

- Administrators, curriculum specialists, and other support staff must reserve time to attend all formal training sessions. No excuses for lack of participation are satisfactory. They can not give the kind of constructive feedback necessary if they are not intimately familiar with the structure, strategies, and activities.

- Beyond the staff development training days, district and school level instructional leaders must block off adequate time to support the model in classrooms. Active, in-class support is critical to the evolution of the model. See the section of this book entitled "The Role of Administrators" for a checklist designed for each of the four blocks which can be used by administrators in giving feedback to teachers.

The detailed implementation process given for the state-level advocacy can be used for the district plan as well. Lead teachers can be used in the initial training phase or whole faculties can be trained together if enough support can be given to all trainees. Topics to be covered during phases of training would be similar to the ones listed under the state-level training plan. Also, see the chapter in this book entitled, "The Role of the Administrator" for additional ideas of support.

School-Level Support for the 4-Blocks Model

Again, the detailed design of staff development—topics to be covered, credentials of trainers, sufficient time for training and implementation, adequate in-class support with constructive feedback—is similar to that of the state and district planning. The chapter in this book entitled "The Role of the Administrator" was written with the school level administrator in mind. The section includes forms for the use of administrators in offering feedback to teachers. The forms are especially good for administrators who might feel uncomfortable with language arts content.

A FEW WORDS OF CAUTION
about the use of the following pages...

The outline of the 4-Blocks Model offered in this booklet is intended to convey the **basics** of the **primary grade** (1–2) model. The model is not rigidly defined, especially as teachers gain confidence in the delivery and begin to interject more of their own personalities and creativity. However, some elements define the model, provide the careful balance, and ensure a greater level of success.

A **misuse** of this outline would be for teachers to be held by their administrators or by self-imposed standards to rigid, daily compliance with this outline. Instead, this outline is offered in response to those who have asked for more specific details in an attempt to do a better job of getting the model started.

HOW DOES THE 4-BLOCKS CLASSROOM LOOK?

As you look into the classroom, you are likely to see...

- Desks or tables arranged so that students can work in cooperative groups.

- A Word Wall with letters of the alphabet stretching across a wall and with words written on an assortment of colored paper organized under each appropriate letter of the alphabet.

- A pocket chart readily available for a number of activities.

- Student work displayed in the room (as well as elsewhere in the building)—compositions on bulletin boards, student and class-made books on shelves and tables, artwork decorating the walls, etc.

- Charts with vocabulary words clustered by theme or topic. These are words that are valuable for students but which may not be appropriate for the Word Wall.

- An Editor's Checklist written on large chart paper or poster board to be used as a reference for writers as they do their quick editing on rough drafts.

- Books, books, and more books placed in book baskets for Self-Selected Reading, displayed attractively on shelves and window sills, in a class library area, and in other places around the room.

- Other reading materials such as magazines, newspapers, resource materials placed where students can easily access them.

- Environmental print, such as news clippings, signs, cereal boxes, and other packaging that shows evidence that reading has *real world* applications.

- Writing materials in a center or area of the room for students' use. The center will include writing paper in various colors and shapes, stationery and postcards, a stapler, construction paper, glue, crayons, pens, pencils, and maybe computers for composing.

- A carpeted area or rug where students gather close to the teacher for mini-lessons and for read-alouds.

- A timer used by the teacher to assure brisk pacing of each of the blocks.

- Teachers and students engaged in teaching and learning.

GUIDED READING/ BASAL BLOCK

BASIC OUTLINE OF
GUIDED READING/BASAL BLOCK

Major Focus: Building Comprehension and Fluency with Reading;
Exposing Students to a Wide Range of Literature

Total Time: (30–45 minutes)   **Pacing is critical!**

Segment One   (10–15 minutes)

1. Teacher directs a mini-comprehension lesson with whole group of students.

2. Teacher introduces and supports grade-level and easier text in a number of ways over multiple days by
   - building on students' prior knowledge about the text and topic.
   - leading shared, choral, or echo reading.
   - guiding picture discussion and prediction.
   - discussing key vocabulary in context.
   - guiding *Being the Word* or similar support activity.

Segment Two   (15–20 minutes)

1. Teacher provides flexible grouping of all students to read introduced text. Grouping may be paired, individual, teacher reading with a child who needs special assistance, play school groups, or with outside volunteers.

2. Teacher evaluates students' progress (approx. $\frac{1}{5}$ of total class per day) with anecdotal records during this period.

Segment Three: (5–10 minutes)

1. Teacher directs whole group for closure activities which may include
   - discussion of text/literature.
   - acting out the story.
   - writing in response to reading.
   - discussion of application, discovery, and transfer of skill or strategy introduced in Segment One mini-lesson.

TEACHER'S 4-BLOCKS INSTRUCTIONAL
SELF-ASSESSMENT INSTRUMENT

Guided Reading/Basal Block

In preparing and presenting my lesson in this block, I have...

_____ 1. Selected a skill or strategy to introduce in my mini-lesson that is necessary to improve reading comprehension.

_____ 2. Introduced new material by previewing pictures and making predictions.

_____ 3. Allowed students several opportunities to practice and make approximations through my modeling and through shared and choral reading before their first attempt to read aloud individually.

_____ 4. Provided grade level or easier material for this block.

_____ 5. Used either basals, multiple copies of tradebooks, and/or big books.

_____ 6. Assisted students in making connections between the content and what is familiar prior to reading (established prior knowledge).

_____ 7. Varied the genre of instructional materials/texts presented in multiple days during this block.

_____ 8. Established and stated a clear purpose for students' reading during the flexible grouping segment.

_____ 9. Provided consistent models of the types of higher level questions that students should ask of themselves, partners, and literary circles during and after reading.

_____ 10. Arranged grouping during Segment Two that is flexible and purposeful. If at all possible, readers who need greater levels of support are paired with stronger readers. No grouping remains stagnant or easily identifiable, especially with weak readers.

Guided Reading/Basal Block
Errors, Misunderstandings, and Weaknesses
Most Commonly Observed in Early Implementation

1. Teachers who are not yet convinced that the model can be effective as designed during Segment Two of the block tend to continue with the traditional three reading groups instead during that period of time or to provide groupings such as playschool that revert to traditional reading groups. They often express anxiety about their redefined role and perceive it as being less "in control" of the lesson. The 4-Blocks Model, however, ensures that students have more actual reading time and that they attend more closely to the text than in the traditional structure.

2. Teachers often confuse the primary purpose of the Guided Reading Block which is to improve comprehension. Other Blocks provide a more appropriate context for skills instruction such as phonics, grammar, and mechanics.

3. Many teachers attempt to implement the Block without the necessary support of adequate and appropriate materials. **Schools must provide adequate supplies of grade level and easier texts for this block.**

4. Round-robin reading (when students take turns reading aloud to a group without benefit of practicing text) is **not** a part of this model.

A Glance at a Typical Week's Lessons For the Guided Reading/Basal Block

Monday	**Grade Level Story:** *Flower Garden* **by Eve Bunting (Harcourt Brace Jovanovich, 1994)**

Segment 1
- Activating Prior Knowledge: Teacher shares a flower from her own garden and some of her personal experience with gardens and asks kids about their experience.
- Teacher conducts picture walk through the book, pointing out key vocabulary.
- Mini-Lesson: Plot/Sequence of Events – Teacher explains that a characteristic of narrative text is that it has a plot (sequence of events) which is important to the story.
- Teacher invites students to join in a shared reading of the story.
- Purpose for paired reading: read same text with partner. When finished, try to retell the major events of plot to partner in correct sequential order

Segment 2
- Students read story in assigned pairs.
- As pairs finish, they attempt to retell events of story to each other.
- Teacher monitors certain students and makes anecdotal notes.

Segment 3
- Students retell major events of story in whole group as teacher records events on sentence strips and places in pocket chart. Teacher closes block with surprise that students will be learning more about plants and seeds in science and will have an opportunity to plant some flowers and vegetables!

Tuesday	**Grade Level Story (Cont.):** *Flower Garden* **by Eve Bunting**

Segment 1
- Activating Prior Knowledge: Teacher reads sentence strips of major events of plot from previous day and then invites students into shared reading of the sentence strips.
- Mini-Lesson: Teacher rearranges sentence strips in pocket chart and reads to students.
- Teacher poses question: Does the order of the events make a difference to the story? Discussion.
- Teacher leads students through choral reading of most of the story.
- Teacher sets purpose for paired reading: After reading the story together, pairs should work together to put events of plot in correct order (same simple sentences from prior day's plot summary but written on paper and cut into strips for each pair of students).

Segment 2
- Teacher monitors certain students to make anecdotal notes of their progress. Students read in pairs. As they finish, they work together to put sentences in correct order.

Segment 3
- In whole group, students check their efforts at arranging sentence strips in correct order of plot with the arrangement provided by the teacher. Students conclude that the sequence of events is important in a story.

Wednesday   Grade Level Story (Cont.): *Flower Garden* by Eve Bunting

Segment 1 • Teacher activates prior knowledge: Reviews briefly what students discovered this week about the important order of the events of a story. Talks a little about the beautiful pictures in the story and the illustrator who drew them. Also, some favorite illustrators of the class members are mentioned.

        • Mini-Lesson: Teacher explains how good readers use picture clues to help them understand the story. Teacher reads several pages of the story and relates pictures to comprehension. A couple of times the teacher models mental pictures created even when no pictures are on the page.

        • After a few pages of modeling the use of picture clues, the teacher invites students to choral read.

        • Teacher states purpose for paired reading: Read together, and then when timer sounds students will have a few minutes to talk about how they would act out the story they have read.

Segment 2 • Students read with assigned pairs with the exception of a small group of three children with whom the teacher wants to work. (Two of them are struggling a bit with the plot concept. The third does not have a partner and makes a good addition to the small group). The small group does a shared reading with the teacher. After 10 minutes the timer sounds and the teacher reminds students to talk for a few minutes about how this story could be acted out.

Segment 3 • Teacher organizes several students to improvise the story as she reads. Prior to acting, teacher asks: See if this play is at all what you pictured when you read the story.

Thursday   New Story from Easier Material: *Growing Vegetable Soup* by Lois Ehlert (Harcourt Brace Jovanovich, 1987)

Segment 1 • Teacher establishes prior knowledge: Teacher leads class to recall what they have learned this week about gardens and gathers their recollections on a graphic organizer (web). Also, shares a garden tool (hoe) and tells how useful it is. Adds tools in one area of the web.

        • Mini-lesson: Uses graphic organizer (topic web) to show relationships of key words.

        • Teacher does picture walk of big book exploring story's key words.

        • Teacher reads big book to class.

        • Teacher states purpose for paired reading: Do a picture walk with your partner and see if you are able to match pictures with labeled words on the page. (This is particular to this book.)

Segment 2 • Assigned pairs of students work in multiple little copies of the same title as the big book by matching words and pictures that surround text on the pages.

        • Teacher monitors certain students as they work and makes anecdotal notes of the strategies they use.

Segment 3 • With all students gathered, teacher elicits words from students and adds appropriately to the original graphic organizer (web) used at the beginning of class.

Segment 1 • Teacher activates learning and establishes prior knowledge by returning to the graphic organizer from the previous day. Together with class she reviews the words listed and the relationship of those words to the concept of gardening.

         • Mini-Lesson: The graphic organizer is used both as the mini-lesson and to link with prior knowledge.

         • Teacher leads shared reading using big book.

         • Teacher states purpose for today's reading with partners: As you read and when you have finished, think of words that we might add to our graphic organizer and decide where the words will need to go (categorizing under correct heading).

Segment 2 • Students read individual copies of little books with assigned partners.

         • Teacher monitors targeted students and makes anecdotal notes of their progress.

Segment 3 • In whole group, teacher lets students volunteer new words to add to the graphic organizer and under which heading they think the word should be placed. At conclusion, teacher tells students that this same graphic organizer will be used to gather information with many topics which they will study.

The teacher may consider some of the following activities to connect the theme of study from the literature read in these guided reading lessons to other blocks and to other content areas:

• Construct a Making Words lesson using a concept word from the stories, such as the word *garden*.

• Pull some of the high frequency words for the Word Wall from the story, such as *get, us, great, look, their*.

• Use the same graphic organizer (topic map) again as pre-writing mini-lesson.

• Plant seeds in science class.

• Write and illustrate in journals daily or weekly about their own observation of the seeds they plant.

• Plan a butterfly garden for the school courtyard.

• Try Lois Ehlert's signature art in illustrating the class experience at planting a garden.

• Make a window box of paper and fill with paper flowers in art class.

• Work on a class project to surprise the school secretary with a window box of flowers on his or her birthday just as the girl did in the story. Construct a class book about this project to give the secretary with her gift. Use math skills of measurement to construct the box.

• Research whether the flowers shown in the *Flower Garden* are grown in their own area.

• Research which insects, birds, and butterflies are attracted by which plants.

BASIC CLASSROOM SUPPLIES
FOR THE GUIDED READING/BASAL BLOCK

✓ Multiple copies of a variety of grade level basals or other quality literature of various genres

✓ Multiple copies of a variety of easier (than grade level) reading materials in various genres

✓ Big books with corresponding multiple class copies of the same titles

✓ Easel for ease in reading big books

✓ Pocket chart

✓ Lots of sentence strips

✓ Record keeping system (can be constructed using file folders, note cards, and tape; or by using a notebook) [see pages 46–50 on *assessment*]

✓ A curriculum guide that provides comprehension skills and strategies that are important for this grade level

SELF-SELECTED READING BLOCK

BASIC OUTLINE OF
SELF-SELECTED READING BLOCK

Major Focus:	**Building Fluency in Reading;** **Allowing Students to Work with Text Most Appropriate to Their** **Own Independent Reading Levels;** **Building Confidence in Students as Readers**

Total Time: (25–40 minutes)

Segment One   (5–10 minutes)

1. Teacher reads aloud to all students, including a variety of fiction and non-fiction, topics, and authors.

Segment Two   (15–20 minutes)

1. Students choose a book from the book baskets at their tables to read independently in one of three ways which have been modeled by the teacher:
   - Students read the words—*real* reading.
   - Students read the pictures in a picture walk through the book.
   - Students retell familiar stories to themselves.

2. The teacher holds conferences with designated children daily as all children are reading and keeps a conference form or anecdotal record of the children's individual progress in independent reading.
   - Students may read aloud several paragraphs or pages to the teacher.
   - Students may tell or retell the story, or may talk about the pictures.
   - Teacher may ask questions about story elements, likes or dislikes, etc.

Segment Three   (5–10 minutes)

1. One or two students share briefly (approximately 2 minutes) what they have read with all students gathered, if possible, on floor near the student who is seated in the Reader's Chair.

2. The reader answers several questions from classmates about the story if time allows. Teachers model the types of thoughtful questions they want students to ask of each other.

TEACHER'S 4-BLOCKS INSTRUCTIONAL SELF-ASSESSMENT INSTRUMENT

Self-Selected Reading Block

In preparing and presenting my lesson in this block, I have...

_____ 1. Provided a good model of fluency in reading and have attempted to motivate students through a teacher read-aloud daily. My read-aloud was clear, expressive, and enthusiastic.

_____ 2. Modeled the three ways that students can read independently during self-selected reading time.

_____ 3. Provided an adequate supply of books on various topics, of different genre, and on varied reading levels above, below, and on grade level.

_____ 4. Made books easily accessible to children so that they will not lose time in choosing and trading out books.

_____ 5. Equally divided the class so that I know which days I will have conferences with each child.

_____ 6. Limited the time spent on each conference to approximately 3 minutes.

_____ 7. Used questions in my conferences that let children know what is important about their reading rather than emphasizing minor details.

_____ 8. Guided and encouraged children during the conference to read books on appropriate levels and to vary their interests in genre, authors, and topics.

_____ 9. Promoted reading through teacher read-alouds and book talks at several appropriate times throughout the day.

_____ 10. Modeled the types of questions during the block closure time that will lead students to ask thoughtful, important questions about reading.

_____ 11. Connected the teacher read-aloud when possible to a topic or concept which the class has studied or will study.

SELF-SELECTED READING BLOCK
ERRORS, MISUNDERSTANDINGS, AND WEAKNESSES
MOST COMMONLY OBSERVED IN EARLY IMPLEMENTATION

1. Before some teachers realize how powerful this block is, they may feel that it is the least important block and will short-change it. This block is critical for many reasons. Three most important reasons are the following:
   - This is one of the most multi-level of all of the blocks. Those students whose reading levels are above the grade level and easier materials used during the Guided Reading Block must be challenged with more difficult texts during this block.
   - Segment Two is an extremely important time for teachers to work individually with students to assess student's comprehension, to encourage appropriate materials, and to document progress.
   - Independent reading time allows students to see themselves and others as readers.

2. The Self-Selected Reading Block is NOT the same as what has typically been called SSR or DEAR (Drop Everything and Read). It is purposeful and organized beyond most SSR programs. Establishing additional time during the day for a formal independent reading time such as DEAR is unnecessary and may even be counterproductive. Having too much independent time planned during the day may take away from the novelty for students, and teachers may find it difficult for students at the lower grades to stay focused for the additional time.

3. Some schools attempt to implement this block without adequate or appropriate books. **Schools must provide an adequate supply of books for this block. A range of reading levels, topics, and genre are necessary.** As schools build their supply of books, teachers must be resourceful. Some examples of resourcefulness might be the following:
   - Teachers can schedule their Self-Selected Reading Blocks so that book baskets or buckets can be shared room to room.
   - Anthologies or old basals can be separated and bound or stapled into individual stories to be placed in book baskets.
   - Some class or student publications can be included in the book baskets.
   - PTA groups and business partners may wish to purchase books or to give magazine subscriptions. Many support groups want to be asked for specific materials.

4. Some teachers need assistance with conducting a conference for maximum benefits.

A GLANCE AT A TYPICAL WEEK'S LESSONS
FOR THE SELF-SELECTED READING BLOCK

Monday   **Grade Level Story:** *The Carrot Seed* **by Ruth Krauss (Harper & Brothers, 1945)**

Segment 1 • Teacher read-aloud.

Segment 2 • Students make independent selections of books.

• Teacher has a conference with five students (3 minutes each).

• After 20 minutes of reading/conference time, teacher alerts students that reading time has ended and that they should record their books or pages read in their reading logs.

Segment 3 • Two students (selected at random from a deck of index cards with students' names on them) share a brief review and comment on the book they're reading. Each student who shares calls on two students who have questions about the books. After book sharing, students return all books to the book baskets. Students who have not finished their books place their special bookmark in book before returning them to the basket.

Tuesday   **Grade Level Story:** *From Seed to Plant* **by Gail Gibbons (Holiday House, 1991)**

Segment 1 • Teacher read-aloud.
Segment 2 • Same as on Monday.
Segment 3 • Same as on Monday.

Wednesday   **Grade Level Story:** *The Chipmunk Song* **by Joanne Ryder (E.P. Dutton, 1987)**

Segment 1 • Teacher read-aloud.
Segment 2 • Same as on Monday.
Segment 3 • Same as on Monday.

Thursday   **Grade Level Story:** *Air Is All Around You* **by Franklyn Branley (Harper & Row, 1986)**

Segment 1 • Teacher read-aloud.
Segment 2 • Same as on Monday .
Segment 3 • Same as on Monday.

Friday   **Grade Level Story: selected poems from** *Animals Animals* **by Eric Carle (Philomel Books, 1989)**

Segment 1 • Teacher read-aloud. (Teacher chooses animals that fit in with gardening theme.)
Segment 2 • Same as on Monday.
Segment 3 • Same as on Monday.

Basic Classroom Supplies
for the Self-Selected Reading Block

✓ Book basket for each cooperative group of students

✓ Many books of varied genre, topics, and reading levels (approximately 25 books per basket to begin) [see page 25, number 3 for examples of sources for books]

✓ Book logs for each student

✓ Record keeping system, including conference forms (can use file folders with conference forms)

✓ Books appropriate for teacher read-alouds

WORKING WITH WORDS BLOCK

BASIC OUTLINE OF
WORDS BLOCK

Major Focus: Enabling children to read, spell, and use high-frequency words correctly; Establishing the patterns necessary for decoding and spelling.

Total Time: (30–40) minutes   Pacing is <u>especially</u> critical!

Segment One   (10–15 minutes)

1. Teacher introduces 5 Word Wall words per week by having students:
   - see the words.
   - say the words.
   - chant the words (snap, clap, stomp, cheer, etc.).
   - write the words and check them together with the teacher.
   - trace around the words and check together with the teacher.
   - complete *On the Back* activities involving the words.

2. On days of the week when new Word Wall words are not the focus, teacher reviews previous Word Wall words using various activities, including but not limited to *Review Cross-Checking, Be a Mind Reader, Wordo* or other activities which reinforce the use and understanding of these high frequency words.

Segment Two   (20–25 minutes)

Teacher guides activities to help children learn spelling patterns. Activities may include:
- *Making Words* in which children manipulate letters of alphabet to construct words from word families. (Suggested at least twice a week.)
- *Sorting Words*, connected to *Making Words*, emphasizes word parts rather than individual letters to establish patterns and relationships among words and word families.
- *Guess the Covered Word*, which is a modified Cloze activity.
- *Rounding Up the Rhymes*, which emphasizes spelling and rhyming patterns.
- Other activities that teach and reinforce the patterns of spelling.

TEACHER'S 4-BLOCKS INSTRUCTIONAL SELF-ASSESSMENT INSTRUMENT

Words Block

In preparing and presenting my lesson in this block, I have...

_____ 1. Introduced only words for the Word Wall which are used frequently in reading and writing at this grade and which should be spelled and used correctly.

_____ 2. Provided a good written and spoken model of the correct spelling and pronunciation of each of the Word Wall words.

_____ 3. Found ways—other than the Word Wall—to display words other than high-frequency ones that students will want to use in their writing, and have meaningfully clustered them (color charts, theme charts) for easy access.

_____ 4. Planned activities beyond Word Wall that help students explore words and transfer their learning to other materials that they read and write.

_____ 5. Made the Making Words activity multi-level by allowing students the opportunity to build up to bigger words.

_____ 6. Planned each Making Words activity so that patterns are clearly and purposefully established by always building on a word or word part. If students "wipe the slate clean" each time they make a word, these patterns will not be clear. I have directed this activity so that students are not merely "playing with" letters.

_____ 7. Connected the "big word" in Making Words to a concept or topic studied when possible.

_____ 8. Briskly paced my Making Words lesson by not waiting for each child to correctly spell the given word before sending a student to the chart to share the correct spelling with the class. Then, I have encouraged all students to check and spell correctly. This way advanced students will not grow impatient.

_____ 9. Sorted for a variety of patterns in my Making Words lessons.

_____10. Transferred sorted rhymes and patterns to read and spell a few new words.

_____11. Correlated the sorting patterns with curricular objectives.

WORDS BLOCK
ERRORS, MISUNDERSTANDINGS, AND WEAKNESSES
MOST COMMONLY OBSERVED IN EARLY IMPLEMENTATION

1. **Often teachers will put words other than high frequency words** (grade appropriate words which are used frequently in what is read and written and which should always be used and spelled correctly) **on the Word Wall. This wall must be used ONLY for high frequency words. Other words can be placed on thematic or cluster charts displayed in the room.** One exception might be placing students' names on the Word Wall to begin the year.

2. Some teachers may not realize the impact of the mere organization of their Word Wall. These are reminders that are sometimes necessary:
   - As much as possible, they should display the letters of the alphabet from left to right, NOT in short, broken columns or misaligned rows which cause students to hunt unnecessarily for the letters. Many students are still learning the alphabet and are confused by erratic order.
   - The Word Wall should be placed where all students can see it with little or no effort. Students should not have to stand, turn backwards, or leave their seats to see it.
   - The letters and words displayed on the Word Wall should be legibly written and large enough to see at a distance.
   - Most, if not all, words on the Word Wall will be in lower case letters. Random capitalization will confuse students.
   - Word Wall words should be carefully cut into shapes of their outlines to provide valuable configuration cues for students.

3. Often teachers will not organize the Making Words activity so that the spelling patterns are clear to students. Remember these points:
   - **The teacher should always direct the construction of words.** For example, teachers should NOT say, "Using the letters I've given you, see what two letter words you can make." Rather, the teacher might say, **"Using one pink letter (vowels) and one white letter (consonants), make the word *it*."**
   - **The teacher should direct students to move from one word to another by having the students keep some remaining letters on the slate from the last word spelled.** For example, a teacher might say, "Take off just one letter from the word *man* and add a letter that would make the word *tan*," then progressing to the boy's name *Stan* and then to the word *stand*. **Establishing those spelling patterns for future transfer is the primary purpose of Making Words.**

4. Some teachers will tend to wait for each child in the room to make every word before sharing the correct spelling. **Pacing should be brisk enough to keep all students engaged.**

A Glance at a Typical Week's Lessons For the Words Block

Monday

Segment 1 • Teacher introduces 5 new Word Wall words: *get, us, great, look, their.* As each new word is introduced, students see the word, say the word, chant the word, write the word, trace the word, and check words with the teacher. Then teacher leads *On the Back* activities.

Segment 2 • Teacher leads the students in a *Making Words* activity, using theme word *flowers* as the big word. Teacher guides students through words 1-11 (see chart), holding off on the big word for a later day.

Tuesday

Segment 1 • Teacher reviews the five new Word Wall words for the week and a few old Word Wall words using *Be a Mind Reader* activity.

Segment 2 • Teacher returns to the Making Words activity from Monday and uses the eleven words to do a variety of sorting activities for patterns that are useful in writing and reading.

Wednesday

Segment 1 • Teacher reviews old Word Wall words by leading a game of Wordo with a playing board of 9 words.

Segment 2 • Teacher leads the class in a *Making Words* activity using different words made from the same letters used on Monday (See words *a-h* on the chart), revealing the big theme word, *flower.* Teacher then proceeds with a brief sorting activity.

Thursday

Segment 1 • Teacher leads the class in *Be a Mind Reader* activity with week's new words and 5 review words, having students write the words. Teacher chooses a few of the words that are pattern words to have students do a transfer exercise as an *On the Back* activity.

Segment 2 • Teacher reads story with rhyming words and plays *Rounding Up the Rhymes.*

Friday

Segment 1 • Teacher leads class members in an informal assessment by having them write the 5 new Word Wall words and 5 review words and then does an *On the Back* activity to see if students are able to transfer patterns to other words they will need in reading and writing.

Segment 2 • Teacher leads the class in *Guess the Covered Word* using sentences and words that fit into the week's theme (Examples: Mrs. Randall grows ***** in her garden.)

PLANNING THE MAKING WORDS LESSON AROUND A THEME

Steps a teacher may use to plan a Making Words Lesson:

1. Teacher chooses a key word or two consisting of six or seven letters related to the theme under study. (Example: **gardens, flowers**)

2. Teacher uses a Spelling Ace™ or similar gadget (convenient but not essential) to generate a menu of words from which lessons are planned according to patterns. (70 words generated for **gardens**; 57 words for **flowers**)

3. Teacher arranges the list according to the number of letters in the words. (Each list with 2–7 letters)

4. Teacher eliminates words which may not be appropriate for grade level, and considers the words that are appropriate. (Words such as *gar, floes, erg* are not familiar nor are they likely needed for writing or reading. Boldfaced words on charts on the next two pages are those being considered by the teacher.)

5. Teacher studies obvious rhyming patterns, phonetic skills, etc., available in the use of certain words. For example: using spelling and rhyming patterns (**rag, nag, sag**, ...), rearranging the same letters (**range** → **anger**), adding suffixes (**lose** → **loser**), or exploring homonyms (**rose/rows/roes, so/sew/sow**).

6. Teacher decides which words provide opportunities to teach the patterns, skills, etc. that the teacher feels are most beneficial to the students and which cover necessary curricular objectives.

7. Teacher starts with 2-letter words and plans logical sequence of patterns, building from one word to the next by adding a letter or rearranging letters (For example: **so** → **sow** → **row** → ...). Teacher includes a balance of easy, average, and difficult words which challenge all students (For example: so, row, flow, slower, flowers).

PLANNING FOR MAKING WORDS

THEME WORD: gardens

Possible Combinations of Letters

2	3	4	5	6	7
ad (1)	age	aged	anger (9)	danger (10)	gardens (11j)
an (2) (a)	and (3)	dare	grade (g)	gander	dangers
	are	darn	grand (f)	ranged	ganders
	den (5)	dean	raged	garden (i)	
	ear	dear (6)	range (8) (e)	angers	
	end (4)	drag	dares	grades (h)	
	era	earn	darns	ranges	
	erg	gear (7)	deans	sander	
	gad	near	dears	snared	
	gar	nerd	degas		
	nag	rage (d)	drags		
	rag (c)	read	dregs		
	ran (b)	ages	earns		
	red	dens	gears		
	sag	ears	rages		
	Dan	ends	reads		
	Ned	eras	sedan		
	gas	ergs	snare		
		nags			
		rags			
		sand			

Obvious Sorting Patterns:

plurals, short *a*, long *a*, -*ag* pattern, -*ed* endings, *r* controlled vowels, -*an* pattern, -*er* endings

Boldface Words = Words considered by teacher in planning (then some of these words will be discarded or not used in lesson.)

1 - 11 = First day's sequence for *Making Words*

a - j = Second day's sequence for *Making Words*

PLANNING FOR MAKING WORDS

THEME WORD: flowers

Possible Combinations of Letters

2	3	4	5	6	7
so (1)	**elf (a)**	**flew**	flews	flower	**flowers (13h)**
	few	**flow (7)**	floes	fowler	fowlers
	foe	floe	**flows (9)**	**lowers (12)**	
	for	**foes**	**fowls**	**slower (11)**	
	fro	fore	**loser (f)**		
	low (3)	**fowl**	**lower (g)**		
	ore	**lore**	roles		
	owe	**lose**	sower		
	owl	**lows**	**swore**		
	ref	ores	**worse (e)**		
	roe	**owes**	slows (10)		
	row (4)	**owls**			
	sew	**refs**			
	sow (2)	roes			
		role			
		rose (6)			
		rows (5)			
		self (b)			
		serf			
		slew			
		slow (8)			
		sole			
		sore			
		woes			
		wolf (c)			
		wore (d)			

Obvious Sorting Patterns:

long *o*, homonyms, *–ore* rhyme, *fl–* blend, *–lf*, *–ow* rhyme, *–ower* rhyme, *–er* ending

Boldface Words	=	Words considered by teacher in planning (then some of these words will be discarded or not used in the lesson.)
1 - 13	=	First day's sequence for *Making Words*
a - h	=	Second day's sequence for *Making Words*

PLANNING FOR MAKING WORDS

THEME WORD:

Possible Combinations of Letters

2	3	4	5	6	7

Sorting Patterns:

BASIC CLASSROOM SUPPLIES
FOR THE WORD BLOCK

✓ Construction paper or cardstock in a wide variety of colors (approximately 50 sheets to be cut in thirds) for Word Wall words

✓ Extra-wide black felt marker

✓ Pocket chart

✓ Sentence strips

✓ Lots of index cards (large and small)

✓ Clasp envelopes (approximately 40 in the 7" x 10" size)

✓ First grade paper (cut in half sheets) for use daily with each student

✓ Red pens or pencils for checking and tracing around Word Wall words

✓ Sets of consonants (2 of each per student) printed on cardstock

✓ Sets of vowels (2 of each per student) printed on cardstock

✓ Some organizer for storing and distributing Making Words letters—utility cabinet, sandwich baggies, or sewn cards, etc.

✓ Material for students to use in framing words at their desks during Making Words—folder, felt strips, etc.

WRITING BLOCK

BASIC OUTLINE OF
WRITING BLOCK

Major Focus:	**Building Fluency in Writing; Employing the Writing Process; Refining and Applying Knowledge of Phonics; Building Confidence as a Writer**

Total Time:	**(30–40 minutes)**	**Pacing is critical!**

Segment One   (10 minutes)

1. Teacher presents a mini-lesson in which he or she models *real* writing for class and a skill or strategy to be emphasized.
   - Mini-lesson focuses on writing a piece, adding on to a piece, or editing a piece.
   - Teacher refers to the Word Wall, lightning words, and other charts in room to model the use of available resources.
   - Teacher models the use of an Editor's Checklist chart which has been developed to promote and guide self-checking and peer editing. This checklist grows as appropriate expectations are added throughout the year.

Segment Two   (15–20 minutes)

1. Students write on self-generated topics, individually paced at various stages of the writing process, perhaps working for multiple days on one piece.

2. Individual editing conferences occur between student and teacher while other students write. In conference, teacher and student pick one piece among 3-4 good pieces of writing to edit for publication.

3. The teacher may present an option of several choices for students during the last 5 minutes of this segment:
   - Continue to write.
   - Share what has been written with a peer.
   - Illustrate what has been written.

Segment Three   (5–10 minutes)

1. Selected students will share briefly (approximately 2 minutes) what they have written with all students gathered, if possible, on floor near reader who is seated in the Author's Chair.

2. The "author" answers several questions from classmates about the writing. Teachers model the types of thoughtful questions they want students to ask of each other.

Teacher's 4-Blocks Instructional Self-Assessment Instrument

Writing Block

In preparing and presenting my lesson in this block, I have...

_____ 1. Selected a skill or strategy to introduce in my mini-lesson that is necessary to improve writing skills.

_____ 2. Provided a good model of writing, though not so sophisticated that students feel they cannot attain a similarly good piece of writing.

_____ 3. Modeled extending a piece of writing by beginning a piece one day and continuing to write on the same piece the next day.

_____ 4. Allowed students to generate their own topics of interest. Here they will learn that writing is telling and that everyone has something to tell.

_____ 5. Modeled the use of resources in the room which are readily available to students—Word Wall, lightning word chart, as well as other charts and pictures.

_____ 6. Modeled how a student might "stretch-out" a word which serves to build fluency in writing, to demonstrate application of phonics knowledge, and to de-emphasize correctness of spelling at the rough draft stage of writing.

_____ 7. Varied the purpose and audience of my writing over numerous lessons.

_____ 8. Provided models of the types of higher level questions that students should ask of themselves and of their peers about writing.

_____ 9. Provided clear criteria to students about what is considered a good piece of writing.

_____10. Provided motivation for writing through several avenues of publishing such as making a book, displaying work in the classroom or halls, or sharing over e-mail with another class.

_____11. Provided an Editor's Checklist chart to assist students with self- and peer editing of their work. The criteria on this chart grow appropriately as children develop in their writing.

Writing Block
Errors, Misunderstandings, and Weaknesses
Most Commonly Observed in Early Implementation

1. **Some teachers fail to use the Segment One modeling time to deliver a mini-lesson. Both the modeling of writing and explicit writing instruction are necessary.**

2. The modeling time and mini-lesson should not overemphasize correctness of conventions (spelling, grammar, and mechanics) in the rough draft stage. The use of the Editor's Checklist should be brief and should concentrate on basics.

3. Some teachers remain convinced that writing topics must always be assigned. **However, students write best about what they are passionate or excited about.** Teachers should not make the assumption that students will not write without being told what to write after only trying the student-generated writing a couple of times. Establishing habits and setting expectations will ensure that this block can be successful.

4. Teachers should not produce such stellar, sophisticated examples during their model lessons that students feel that such writing standards are unattainable.

5. Some teachers tend to short-change or even to eliminate the sharing during Segment Three. **Sharing is critical to success both in motivating students to write and in encouraging discussions from the viewpoints of authors.**

6. Some teachers hesitate to publish students' work or wait until the last few weeks of school to attempt publication. **A valuable motivational tool is lost if publishing is not begun early in the year and continued at regular intervals.** This also provides greater opportunity to teach the entire writing process.

A Glance at a Typical Week's Lessons
For the Writing Block

Monday

Segment 1 • Teacher invites students to come and sit in a semi-circle around the area of the overhead projector. Teacher shows students a new pack of stationery that she has just purchased. She mentions the types of notes that she writes most often to different people. She says that one note that she needs to write now is a thank-you note to her neighbor for feeding and caring for her dog while she was away for the weekend. She says that she will plan what to say as her writing lesson for that day. She sits on a chair beside the overhead project and begins to write a draft of her thank-you note. As she writes, she models how a first grader would "stretch out" a word that he was unsure how to spell. After writing several good sentences that compose a complete note, she rereads her note and then checks the items on the Editor's Checklist to see if she has remembered the basics. Then she says that she will use that draft to write her card. The mini-lesson is on letter writing format.

• While students are still sitting in the semi-circle, teacher asks students where they will be starting in their writing process that day. Some students report that they will be starting a new piece; some will be working on a second or third day of the same piece; some will be illustrating a piece which they have already edited with the teacher; and several are ready for a conference with the teacher. After planning, the teacher dismisses students to proceed with their writing.

Segment 2 • Students work on compositions at various stages.

• Teacher has individual conferences with three students who are ready to edit a good piece of their writing before publication.

• Teacher gives a signal to let students know they have five minutes remaining and that they can make one of three choices: 1) continue to write, 2) illustrate what they have written, or 3) share their work with a peer.

Segment 3 • Three students are selected to share their writing with the class in the author's chair. Other class members come to sit around the author's chair to listen. After each student reads, a couple of classmates get to tell what they like about the writing and ask questions about it. The teacher asks a good question to model to the students the kinds of thoughtful questions she hopes students will ask and will think about in their writing.

Tuesday

Segment 1 • Teacher invites students to come and sit in a semi-circle around the area of the overhead projector. She shares that she wants to tell them about an experience she once had planting a garden since they are reading about and studying about planting that week. Her story deals with planting a garden only to have squirrels come right behind her and dig it all up again. The kids laugh at the story. The teacher ties in the mini-lesson to what the students are learning in Guided Reading Block—sequencing a story.

• While students are still sitting in the semi-circle, teacher asks students where they will be starting in their writing process that day. Lesson continues as on Monday.

Segment 2 • Same as Monday.

Segment 3 • Same as Monday.

Wednesday

Segment 1 • Teacher invites students to come and sit in a semi-circle around the area of the overhead projector. Teacher uses a graphic organizer to get her thoughts together to write today. She wants to summarize in "report style" what the class has learned so far about plants and gardening. She draws a topic map and the different areas she wants to cover. She adds some details under each of three areas. Tomorrow she will begin to write using this graphic organizer to guide her writing.

• Same as Monday with circle planning.

Segment 2 • Same as Monday.

Segment 3 • Same as Monday.

Thursday

Segment 1 • Teacher invites students to come and sit in a semi-circle around the area of the overhead projector. Teacher uses the previous day's graphic organizer (topic map) to begin writing an expository piece on what they have learned about plants and gardening. She is able to cover two of the three main areas and says that she will continue tomorrow. She uses the Editor's Checklist for a quick check on the writing already completed. She emphasizes staying on topic with all sentences.

• While students are still sitting in the semi-circle, teacher asks students where they will be starting in their writing process that day and lesson continues as on Monday.

Segment 2 • Same as Monday.

Segment 3 • Same as Monday.

Friday

Segment 1 • Teacher invites students to come and sit in a semi-circle around the area of the overhead projector. Teacher uses the previous day's graphic organizer (topic map) to continue writing an expository piece on what they have learned about plants and gardening. She is able to complete the composition and uses the Editor's Checklist for a quick check. She, again, emphasizes staying on topic with all sentences.

 • Planning is the same as preceding days.

Segment 2 • Same as Monday.

Segment 3 • Same as Monday.

BASIC CLASSROOM SUPPLIES AND EQUIPMENT FOR THE WRITING BLOCK

✓ Overhead projector

✓ Lined transparencies (using the lines appropriate for the grade level)

✓ "Gathering space" in the room, preferably on a rug or a carpeted area

✓ Writing and publishing materials (different types of writing paper, cardstock for covers, bindings or staplers, scissors, pencils, pens, crayons and/or paints—and a computer would be great!)

✓ Individual student folders or notebooks

✓ Poster board for Editor's Checklist

Q & A
ON
ASSESSMENT

46

What valid measure can a school or teacher use to assess the growth of individual children in the area of reading comprehension?

For schools and teachers concerned about having a valid measure of growth, especially at grades where state testing is not mandated, an Informal Reading Inventory (IRI) can be administered. This instrument can offer teachers, schools, and districts some standardized measure to accurately assess growth of individual students and to gather valuable information about individual strengths and weaknesses in decoding and comprehension that can be used effectively to plan more individualized instruction. The IRI is administered individually to students as a pre and post measure or at any interval when analytical data is needed.

How can school personnel learn to administer IRIs?

Many undergraduate students learn to administer IRIs in their college education classes. A course, however, is not necessary. Anyone who is knowledgeable about this assessment method can teach others. Teachers and administrators can be easily trained to administer IRIs and to glean helpful information from the data. Learning this instrument is not difficult but does require some practice. There are many good IRIs available on the market for purchase. Also, they come complete with the testing materials necessary for a wide range of grades (pre-primer through grade 8 and above) and with the instructions for administration of the test.

Who can administer the IRIs with so many students needed to be assessed?

Almost anyone who is willing to be trained and who has some practice time can administer an IRI. Teachers are probably the most ideal test administrators because their students know them and feel comfortable with them. Also, administering IRIs offers a perfect opportunity for teachers to gain a depth of knowledge about the reading ability of their students. However, there are many effective and efficient ways for the IRIs to be administered. Some districts or schools construct a team of people (administrators, guidance counselors, media specialists, instructional assistants, curriculum specialists, and willing, trained parent volunteers) to administer the IRIs so that instructional time will not be interrupted in classrooms.

When can IRIs be administered?

Because IRIs offer several forms of the test, they can be used as pre and post testing for the school year and can be used at intervals when additional analytical data is needed for individual students. Teachers can usually find periods of time over several days to assess their own students with the instrument, and many teachers appreciate the first-hand information and the one-to-one interaction of the test situation with their students. Testing should be done as early as possible in the year so that all growth is measured.

Some schools like to test again at the end of the school year, assuming that the measure at that point is more accurate than at the beginning of the next school year with the lapse of two to three months of summer break. Sometimes during the year, a teacher may be puzzled about the lack of progress of several students or may be curious about the rapid growth of some students. Testing for additional information at these intervals is appropriate and could divulge valuable information pertinent to instruction.

How can a teacher construct a portfolio that could be used to gather data about individual student growth, strengths, and weaknesses in the 4-Blocks Model?

A simple beginning for a **student profile portfolio** (Figure C) could be for the teacher to purchase a file folder for each class member. Colorful folders corresponding to purposefully grouped students would be a helpful management tool (for example: Monday students (4)= blue folders; Tuesday students (5) = yellow folders; Wednesday students (5) = green folders; Thursday students (4) = red folders; Friday students (4) = purple folders). The teacher will keep the same colored folders together and can easily identify them when beginning the day's work. If colored file folders are not available, the tabs of the folders could be coded using colored markers. Students' names can be written on the tabs. Several pieces of information can be included on the inside of the folder. On the left inside of the folder, at least one index card for each marking period can be taped in overlapping fashion spaced at vertical intervals. These cards can be used for the anecdotal notes or running records made by teachers during Segment Two of the Guided Reading Block as the teacher monitors predetermined children. To the right inside of the folder, the pre-testing form of the IRI (from the beginning of the school year) can be attached with the conference forms used regularly during Self-Selected Reading Block, stapled for easy access on top of the IRI. Any additional samples such as writing pieces or literature response pieces which the teacher feels reflect typical work of the student can be added to the folder. All of this information completes a profile of the work and progress of the individual student and can be used to plan instruction, to share meaningful information during parent conferences, and to pass to the next grade level teacher for planning.

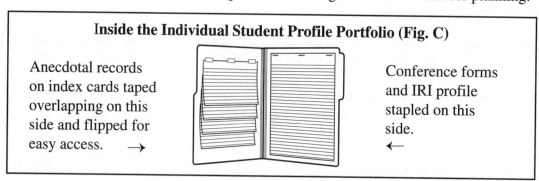

Inside the Individual Student Profile Portfolio (Fig. C)

Anecdotal records on index cards taped overlapping on this side and flipped for easy access. →

Conference forms and IRI profile stapled on this side. ←

What time is provided in the 4-Blocks Model for a teacher to evaluate learning, and what kind of information will a teacher be gathering during those times?

Good teachers, of course, are always observing or "kid-watching" for information that will help to tailor their instruction to individual and class needs. However, there are times during the blocks specifically designated for information gathering as noted below:

Guided Reading/Basal Block—The Segment Two time allows for teachers to monitor the students in the act of reading and completing meaningful tasks with partners. The teacher will be "eavesdropping" on predetermined students and making notes about skills and strategies that apply to comprehension, fluency, and how students encounter various texts and genres. Some questions teachers may be answering during their observations could be: *What primary strategy does the student rely on when he encounters a difficult word? Does a difficult word totally impede the student's reading? How heavily is the student relying upon his partner during reading? Does the student understand that punctuation is an indicator of intonation when reading aloud? Can the student verbalize his task? Are oral skills an obstacle to collaboration with his partner? Does the student appear to need additional help to build prior knowledge about the subject? What kinds of errors are affecting comprehension?*

Self-Selected Reading Block—Again, the Segment Two time allows for teachers to gather information about a student, as an individual conference is held. Teachers will want to select a conference form or design one that helps them to gather and organize information in the short amount of conference time that is provided. Teachers will be able to observe similar types of information as in the Guided Reading Block; however, this one-on-one time may be more directed towards how a student handles a variety of text. Some questions teachers are answering for themselves during this time may be: *Does this student have a sense of what makes a story/narrative? Does the student know how story elements such as character, setting, and plot work together? Is the student reading books that are appropriate for his or her independent reading level? Does the student know how to select an appropriate book for his interest and reading ability? Does the student need to be exposed to other genres?*

Writing Block—The Segment Two period of time allows teachers to work with individual students to select, revise, and edit one good piece of writing. The teacher may want to make notes to include in the profile portfolio of the strengths and weaknesses of a student's writing after working together with the student. The anecdotal notes on index cards would be an appropriate place for these notes or a form could be developed exclusively for the teacher's remarks about the student's writing skills. During the conference time when this information is gathered, a teacher might be focusing on such questions as: *Does the student understand the concept of staying focused in her writing? Does she use simple punctuation correctly? Is she using the Word Wall and other resources in the room during writing? Does she have a sense of what a sentence is? Is she generating different topics or does the teacher need to give her additional assistance in where she might get ideas about what she wants to tell? Is she using the Editor's Checklist for a quick edit after writing a rough draft? Does she demonstrate a basic understanding of phonetic principles? Does the spacing between words and letters indicate that she understands the concept of words and letters? Does the student need to be encouraged to extend a piece of writing over several days? Is the student becoming more confident in her writing?*

Words Block—This block does not provide time for the teacher to be actively engaged in evaluating with note-taking or recording. However, the "kid-watching" will continue as the teacher makes mental notes: *Which students are adept at constructing the spelling patterns and which students are struggling to construct theirs? Which students know a vowel from a consonant? Which students are matching letters and sounds with ease? Which students quickly identify rhyming patterns? Which students make correct guesses when predicting a covered word? Which students should be included in a small group session to have additional exposure to rhyming patterns?*

Can using the 4-blocks model adequately prepare students for state assessments?

Consider the following:

- **The 4-Blocks Model is an instructional delivery system, not a curriculum**. The model is the **way** you will present **what** needs to be taught. Your curriculum needs to be aligned with the testing objectives.

- Reading skills and strategies are fundamental to the 4-Blocks Model. They are taught in the context of real reading and writing and "up close" in focused skills application activities such as *Making Words*.

- There is no need to find time separate and apart from the normal structure of the model to teach the skills included as test objectives. Even test format practice, if desired, can easily fit into the normal flow of the model. For example, *On the Back* activities are ideal for quick practice such as using unfamiliar formats, putting words in alphabetical order, and others; *Word Wall* activities can incorporate practice in such skills as using synonyms and antonyms; the Writing Block mini-lesson and modeling can be the perfect context for reviewing and practicing the kinds of questions and the formatting used in the language section of a test such as MAT7 or other norm referenced tests. Writing rubrics can become several interesting mini-lessons for the Writing Block.

- All skills and strategies can be taught in an interesting, authentic context.

- Keep in mind that **better readers and writers will be better test takers**.

THE

CRITICAL ROLE

OF

ADMINISTRATORS

HOW CAN ADMINISTRATORS FACILITATE AND SUPPORT IMPLEMENTATION OF THE 4-BLOCKS MODEL?

Provide on-going staff development focused on the model and its components.

Too often schools build their staff development for the year around a laundry list of topics, ideas, and programs. Teachers can become overwhelmed by implementing too much. **For the successful implementation of the 4-Blocks Model, teachers need to remain focused on various aspects of the model.** Other content areas are not likely to be slighted; usually teachers and administrators find that the good instructional practices learned through this model transfer into other content areas to improve teaching and learning as well. The model will require that teachers and administrators grow together professionally through the process of studying and absorbing the philosophy that drives the model, through the coaching and practicing that occurs, and through discussions and planning with support networks at grade levels, at the school level, and between and among other schools.

In planning a comprehensive staff development program, administrators should remember that they can take advantage of many opportunities such as:

- Before or after school faculty meetings.
- Monthly faculty study/discussion groups revolving around different topics.
- Weekly grade level meetings.
- Designated staff development days.
- Visits to other schools.

Besides learning the basic model, schools have found it useful to include some of the following topics in further staff development:

- Documenting students' performance through anecdotal note taking.
- Using effective conferencing techniques.
- Administering IRIs.
- Using the IRI to plan instruction.
- Varying activities in the blocks.
- Choosing appropriate mini-lessons in writing.
- Picking appropriate books for teacher read-alouds.
- Relating topics and themes throughout the 4 blocks.
- Making instruction more interdisciplinary.
- Including learning centers in the day.
- Relating the 4-Blocks Model to standards and frameworks.

Be an active participant in the staff development.

Some teachers says that they know what staff development is truly valued by whether or not the principal attends and participates alongside the faculty. Administrators who understand the 4-Blocks Model are able to support it in the classroom by giving constructive feedback.

Plan a budget that includes the materials and equipment necessary for success in each classroom.

Teachers need certain basic materials before they can implement all blocks. Materials lists for each block are included in this booklet. Be resourceful in getting what is needed.

Observe regularly in classes and offer feedback to all teachers.

Regular observations and constructive feedback will encourage teachers to take risks and grow professionally and will communicate expectations of getting the model implemented and strengthened. An introductory form which administrators can use to have teachers invite them into the classroom to observe one block where that teacher feels confident follows this section. If possible, administrators should observe each of the four blocks taught by each teacher at least once throughout the year. An observation checklist for each of the blocks is also included in this booklet. Administrators, even those without a strong background in language arts, will find this checklist approach an easy way to give feedback that should strengthen the model. Also, giving feedback on lesson plans can be helpful, especially as teachers begin to learn to plan for the delivery of the blocks.

Facilitate networks of support for your faculty.

Because there is much to know about this literacy model and because the activities change as the curriculum changes throughout the year, **teachers need networks of support to rely upon to answer the questions they will have at different points.** Principals can encourage grade level and cross grade planning and discussion groups. Additionally, having a partner school with which teachers can communicate about successes and failures can be a real asset.

Plan the schedule to accommodate the model.

Sometimes schedules are obstacles to the success of the model. If your expectation is that the model is to be implemented, have the schedule accommodate the model so that every teacher is not working needlessly to accommodate the schedule. Teachers must have a minimum of 2-1/4 to 2-1/2 hours of total language arts time. The blocks do not necessarily have to be consecutive; however, four 30-40 minute chunks of time are ideal. Also, providing grade level planning time at least one time per week and encouraging teachers to use that time together effectively is a tremendous time-saver for teachers.

Name _____   Date _____

Grade Level _____

ADMINISTRATOR'S/COACH'S OBSERVATION CHECKLIST
FOR THE
GUIDED READING/BASAL BLOCK

The following items are key elements of the Guided Reading Block which occur daily and which are observable. This does not include all activities of this block.

	1	2	3
Teacher uses grade level or easier material.			
Teacher builds prior knowledge to connect students to text prior to reading.			
Teacher presents a brief mini-lesson on a comprehension skill or strategy.			
Teacher presents or reviews key vocabulary.			
Teacher offers support with text prior to independent reading either by:	███	███	███
Modeling the reading for the students while they track text, **or**			
Leading a shared or choral reading of the text.			
Teacher states purpose for paired or grouped reading assignment.			
Teacher has students grouped in pairs or small flexible groups.			
Teacher provides multiple copies of the text for students.			
Teacher is active during the independent reading time by:	███	███	███
Monitoring targeted students and making anecdotal records, **or**			
Working with individual students or small groups.			
Teacher ensures that all students are engaged in reading.			
Teacher ensures that round-robin reading does not occur.			
Teacher brings whole group back together for closure activity.			
Teacher promotes higher order thinking by posing questions beyond recall.			
Entire block focuses on comprehension (not discrete skills at word or letter level).			
Teacher's classroom management system is conducive to teaching and learning.			
Teacher paces the lesson for 30-40 total minutes.			

1 - No evidence observed.

2 - Evidence suggests that teacher may need additional support and practice.

3 - Observation suggests implementation with understanding.

Comments:

_____

_____

_____

Name _____   Date _____

Grade Level _____

ADMINISTRATOR'S/COACH'S OBSERVATION CHECKLIST
FOR THE
SELF-SELECTED READING BLOCK

The following items are key elements of the Self-Selected Reading Block which occur daily and which are observable. This does not include all activities of this block.

	1	2	3
Teacher reads aloud a selection with enthusiasm and expression.			
Transition into independent reading requires a minimum of movement/noise.			
Independent reading materials are easily accessible to all students.			
Book baskets include books with variety in genre, topics, and reading levels.			
All students are engaged in reading.			
Early emergent readers have learned to "read" pictures with confidence.			
Teacher has individual, brief (approx. 3 min.) conferences with several students.			
Teacher uses a form to record conference information.			
Some brief sharing time brings closure to the block.			
Teacher paces the activities so that the block is 30-40 minutes.			
Teacher's classroom management system is conducive to teaching and learning.			

1 - No evidence observed.

2 - Evidence suggests that teacher may need additional support and practice.

3 - Observation suggests implementation with understanding.

Comments:

_____
_____
_____
_____
_____
_____
_____
_____
_____
_____
_____
_____
_____

Name _____   Date _____

Grade Level _____

ADMINISTRATOR'S/COACH'S OBSERVATION CHECKLIST FOR THE WORD BLOCK

The following items are key elements of the Word Block which occur daily and which are observable. These do not include all activities of this block.

	1	2	3
Teacher introduces or reviews Word Wall (approx. 5 min.).			
Observation of the class Word Wall reveals that			
all letters of the alphabet are in linear, natural progression.			
all words and letters are in legible manuscript.			
all words and letters are large enough to be read easily.			
all words are clearly visible with no obstruction to any student.			
configurations (outline of word shapes) of all words are evident.			
words under each letter vary in color.			
words appear to be those used frequently at this grade level.			
Teacher leads students through correct steps for Word Wall: see the word, say the word, chant the word, write and check, trace around the word and check.			
Teacher provides additional activity or activities during block to teach and support decoding, spelling, and word exploration.			
On days when Making Words activity is done, teacher			
has an efficient system for passing out letters to students.			
clearly emphasizes spelling patterns.			
briskly paces activity.			
keeps all students engaged.			
Teacher helps students understand how knowing spelling patterns will help with other words of similar patterns used in their writing and reading (transfer).			
Teacher paces activity so that block is 30-40 minutes.			
Classroom management system is conducive to teaching and learning.			

1 - No evidence observed.

2 - Evidence suggests that teacher may need additional support and practice.

3 - Observation suggests implementation with understanding.

Comments:

_____

_____

Name _____   Date _____

                                          Grade Level _____

ADMINISTRATOR'S/COACH'S OBSERVATION CHECKLIST
FOR THE
WRITING BLOCK

The following items are key elements of the Writing Block which occur daily and which are observable. This does not include all activities of this block.

	1	2	3
Teacher composes/writes at overhead projector or chart paper.			
During the teacher's writing model, the teacher			
models the use of class resources (Word Wall, charts, etc.)			
emphasizes a writing skill or strategy as mini-lesson, and			
uses the class Editor's Checklist at completion for brief editing.			
Transition into independent writing requires a minimum of disruption.			
Teacher allows students to make choices about independent writing topics.			
Students are in various stages of the writing process during independent time.			
Teacher conferences with some students to discuss a piece of their writing.			
All students are engaged in writing activities.			
As closure activity,			
time is provided for some students to share their writing aloud with the class.			
good speaking skills are encouraged during sharing time.			
teacher encourages higher level, thoughtful questions about composition.			
Class and student publications are displayed in the classroom.			
Teacher's classroom management system is conducive to teaching and learning.			
Teacher paces all activities so the block is 30-40 total minutes.			

1 - No evidence observed.

2 - Evidence suggests that teacher may need additional support and practice.

3 - Observation suggests implementation with understanding.

Comments:

_____

_____

_____

_____

_____

_____

OBSERVATION OF THE 4-BLOCKS CLASSROOMS

Please let me know when I can visit your classroom to observe **one block of the 4-Blocks Model where you feel most comfortable**. Write the name of the block you would like for me to observe and the time and day when I can observe that block. Please notice the times and days where other teachers have requested a visit so that times will not be duplicated.

Week of _____

NAME	BLOCK	MON	TUE	WED	THU	FRI

WHAT SPECIAL OPPORTUNITIES EXIST IN THE MODEL TO ACCELERATE LEARNING FOR THE SLOWEST ACHIEVERS?

Although the model was constructed to address individual differences in learning styles and in varied stages of student achievement, there are numerous appropriate times to give additional help to special needs children as suggested below.

Guided Reading/Basal Block

Segment Two provides ideal time for either the teacher or instructional aide to work with individuals or small, flexible groups of students who need special assistance.

Self-Selected Reading Block

Segment Two provides time for either the teacher or instructional aide to work with individuals or small, flexible groups of students who need special assistance. This focused assistance should be brief enough so that all students are still allowed some independent reading time.

Words Block

Segment One (Word Wall) allows the teacher or instructor's aide to focus on the way that each child learns best (through auditory, visual, or kinesthetic learning or a combination of these.)

Segment Two (during Making Words lessons) provides opportunities for all students, but especially for struggling students, to make building, sorting, and seeing word patterns concrete.

Writing Block

Segment Two provides time for the teacher and/or the instructional aide to tailor instruction to individual children in many ways throughout the writing process as they stretch-out words (application of phonics), revise and refine writing, and as they have students read their own work.

ANNOTATED BIBLIOGRAPHY OF MATERIALS
TO SUPPORT 4-BLOCKS

BOOKS:

Classrooms That Work: They Can All Read and Write. Allington, Richard and Cunningham, Patricia M., Harper Collins College Publishers, 1994.

This is a "must-read" for those who plan to implement the model, although this book does not define the blocks and their components. This book offers the reader not only sound philosophy on which the classroom model is based but also clear classroom portraits and numerous activities and strategies which are integral parts of the 4-Blocks Model of instruction.

Schools That Work: Where All Children Read and Write. Allington, Richard L. and Cunningham, Patricia M., Harper Collins College Publishers, 1996.

Although this book is good reading for all educators, it is especially helpful to administrators and curriculum specialists who need a more comprehensive look at successful school and classroom practices which support the appropriate culture to nourish the 4-Blocks Model.

Phonics They Use. Cunningham, Patricia M., Harper Collins College Publishers, 1995.

This publication is helpful not only for understanding the role of phonics in reading but also for learning the classroom activities and strategies that comprise the Word Block.

Making Words. Cunningham, Patricia M. and Hall, Dorothy P., Good Apple, 1994.

This book explains Making Words, an activity which is essential to the Word Block. Cunningham and Hall assist the reader with implementation of the Word Block by offering many pre-constructed lessons including the patterns for the extended sorting lessons. This book enables readers to construct their own lessons to correlate with themes and concepts being studied.

Making Big Words. Cunningham, Patricia M. and Hall, Dorothy P., Good Apple, 1994.

Identical in format and purpose to *Making Words*, this publication offers bigger, more sophisticated words for use above early primary grades.

No Quick Fix. Allington, Richard L. and Walmsley, Sean, Teachers College Press, 1995.

Although this book describes numerous successful intervention/acceleration programs, one chapter is devoted to the research on implementation of the 4-Blocks and F.R.O.G. Models in North Carolina schools. The research and supporting text are most convincing of the impact made by these models on different populations of students.

Making More Words. Cunningham, Patricia M. and Hall, Dorothy P., Good Apple, 1997.

As a sequel to *Making Words*, this book contains more prepared activities for *Making Words* lessons that will help teachers to make, sort, and transfer appropriate words and patterns with students at the lower elementary grades.

Making More Big Words. Cunningham, Patricia M. and Hall, Dorothy P., Good Apple, 1997.

Just what it says it is—more lessons for teachers using bigger words at the upper grade levels. This will save teachers a great deal of planning time with making, sorting, and transferring appropriate words and patterns.

Month-by-Month Reading and Writing for Kindergarten. Hall, Dorothy P. and Cunningham, Patricia M. (Carson-Dellosa Publ., 1997)

This book includes detailed, easy-to-follow activities to develop phonemic awareness, encourage letter and sound recognition, foster reading and writing skills, and teach essential print concepts.

Month-by-Month Phonics for First Grade. Cunningham, Patricia M. and Hall, Dorothy P. (Carson-Dellosa Publ., 1997)

This book focuses on the **Working with Words Block**, one essential component of the 4-Blocks Literacy Model. The text includes detailed, easy-to-follow activities that help students develop phonemic awareness, enhance letter and sound recognition, and increase vocabulary.

Soon Available: *Phonics and Spelling Through the Year*, Cunningham

VIDEO TAPES:

4-Blocks Model. Cunningham, Patricia M. and Hall, Dorothy P., 1995.

This video was the first publication to clearly delineate the 4 blocks and their essential elements. The tape shows actual classroom demonstrations of each of the blocks with narration by Dr. Cunningham explaining why and how each of the blocks is multi-level and multi-approach for all students. Because the video was funded through a grant, the cost is minimal.

Building Blocks. Cunningham, Patricia M. and Hall, Dorothy, P., 1996.

This video shows a developmentally appropriate adaptation of the 4-Blocks Model for the kindergarten in hopes of offering a foundation that will make students more successful with the 4-Blocks Model in first grade.

Preview Of Videos To Come:

A middle school video is presently being filmed to show appropriate adaptations of the 4-Blocks Model for the upper grades.

SELF-SELECTED READING LOG

STUDENT: _____

DATE	BOOK TITLE	GENRE	LEVEL	TEACHER'S COMMENTS

<u>Genre</u>: fiction, non-fiction, biography, informational, poetry, etc.
<u>Level</u>: easy, appropriate, hard

WRITING LOG ✏️

STUDENT'S NAME: _____

DATE	TOPIC	COMMENTS

NOTES